Curriculum Visions
Dig dee
A dinosaur life
belching, hunting, ferocious, scaly, ruling, gigantic, gruesome, smelly, adventurous, bone-cracking, short, dangerous, exciting...
Dr Brian Knapp

Curriculum Visions

Dig deeper ...

books provide in-depth exploration
into classic popular topics.

... and there's more on-line

You will find multimedia resources
covering a wide range of topics at:

www.CurriculumVisions.com

CurriculumVisions is a subscription web site.

Author
Brian Knapp, BSc, PhD

Senior Designer
Adele Humphries, BA, PGCE

Editor
Gillian Gatehouse

Designed and produced by
Atlantic Europe Publishing

Printed in China by
WKT Company Ltd

A dinosaur life – Curriculum Visions
A CIP record for this book is available from the British Library

Paperback ISBN 978 1 86214 567 2

Picture credits
All photographs and illustrations are from the Earthscape and ShutterStock collections except: (c=centre t=top b=bottom l=left r=right) pages 9, 19tr, 32b, 62l, 62r, *Wikipedia*.

This product is manufactured from sustainable managed forests. For every tree cut down at least one more is planted.

▼ **Utahraptor**

Note on reconstructions

Most of the illustrations are reconstructions by artists based on evidence of what remains of skeletons. The skin colour, texture and so on must, of necessity, be imaginary, which is why other reconstructions done by other artists may look somewhat different, have different colours and so on. Environmental backgrounds are used for effect and to give a sense of scale. They are mainly real environments and may vary in detail from the landscapes that existed at the time of the dinosaurs.

Contents

Note: This book does not attempt to cover all dinosaurs, just give a flavour of the life and times of some of those best known.

Before you turn another page
Imagine creatures from another age
That might awake and give you fright
If you saw them in the middle of the night

You might be faced with gaping jaw
And vicious teeth like you never saw
And horrid belches from deep within
Bringing smells worse than any rubbish bin

One giant stomp from a three-toed foot
Might squash you right where you stood put
And leave no more for friends to see
Than a pancake you might have for tea

How many different kinds of dinosaur poems can you make up? Try to make one for every kind of dinosaur you find in this book.

◀ Nedoceratops (previously called Diceratops), a harmless plant-eating dinosaur, but at 12 tonnes, and galloping at 30 km/hr, it would not have been a beast you would have wanted to get in the way of.

Dinosaurs!

Dinosaurs were **REPTILES** that lived on land between 220 and 65 million years ago and which carried their legs beneath their bodies (picture ①). Flying reptiles – pterosaurs, and ocean-living reptiles – plesiosaurs and ichthyosaurs – were related, but they were not biologically dinosaurs. However, all these dinosaur-like creatures are fascinating and will be included in this book.

Crocodiles and the ancestors of lizards began in this age, but they are also different from dinosaurs; they walk with their legs against the sides of their bodies and have different kinds of bones.

▼ ① A pack of hunting dinosaurs. These were called Aucasaurus. They were not an especially large dinosaur, being just 4 m long and 1 m high at the hip. They weighed 700 kg. In packs, however, they must have been fearsome. Many of Aucasaurus' relatives had bull-like horns. We have no idea what the colour of the skin was. As with all of the dinosaur illustrations you will ever see, therefore, the colours are artist's impressions.

Once, a very, very long time ago

This is the story about the most fantastic creatures that ever lived. They are the dinosaurs and other reptiles that lived between 220 and 65 million years ago. It has been called the 'Age of the Reptiles'.

▲ (1) Dinosaurs may have been given the chance to rule the world by a great catastrophe such as a comet striking the Earth and killing off many other kinds of animal. For 183 million years the dinosaurs 'ruled the Earth', then another catastrophe occurred, the climate changed, the dinosaurs' food ran out, they could not adapt fast enough, and it was then the dinosaurs' time to become extinct.

Let's go back in time. We are now living about 4,600 million years (4.6 billion years) after the Earth first formed. This huge span of time is called geological time (see also page 58). For the first billion years, the Earth's surface was molten, or too hot for life to form. Then an atmosphere with water droplets formed, and slowly water began to build up on the surface to make the oceans. It was in these oceans that life on Earth first started. So, for most of geological time (3,500 million years) there has been some kind of life on Earth, but until a billion years ago or less it was only in the form of tiny single-celled creatures. Then, for reasons that are still unclear, change – **EVOLUTION** – set in quickly.

Life continued in the oceans for hundreds of millions of years, and then some creatures began to develop lungs and live on land. Plants also began to grow on land.

Yet the Earth was not an easy place to live, whether it be on the land or in the sea. From time to time, great natural disasters occurred that affected the whole world. When this happened many of the creatures died out. That is called a mass **EXTINCTION**. But, each time, the remaining creatures were able to thrive and evolve. Indeed, the survivors were often given a chance that they may not have had before. So, from being insignificant creatures, they sometimes became the world's most important creatures.

Perhaps this is how the dinosaurs and similar creatures (which together are called archosaurs by geologists) – the world's largest-ever lizard-like animals – came to develop, for, at the time just before the age of the dinosaurs, there was a terrible natural disaster and most creatures died out (picture ①). A new **GEOLOGICAL AGE** started, called the **TRIASSIC**, and it was during this time that dinosaurs began to rule the world.

The dinosaurs and related animals lived and 'ruled' for an incredible length of time (picture ②). We have been around for about 4 million years. Dinosaurs survived for 183 million years, or nearly fifty times as long as all humankind (so far). Then 65 million years ago, there was another worldwide catastrophe and it was the dinosaurs' time to become mostly **EXTINCT**.

Of course, when you see a crocodile or an alligator, you will know that their relations did not become fully extinct. But although you may not at first realise it, there are millions of dinosaur ancestors, for every modern bird is also descended from the dinosaur.

Dinosaurs were not the only creatures on the Earth. They lived among a huge variety of other creatures, many of which were also spectacular. Some were food for other dinosaurs. Others got their food from plants. And that is why this book is about all the life and times when dinosaurs ruled the Earth.

Dinosaurs have been extinct for 65 million years. So how do we know so much about them? The answer is that their remains were sometimes buried in the ground and preserved. How this happened and how we reconstruct dinosaurs from the bones, we shall see on the following pages.

▼ ② JURASSIC times. In this reconstruction, Europasaurus is the large plant-eater and is with its young. Three Iguanodons (also plant-eaters) are walking by. In the foreground are two turkey-sized Compsognathus, which are hunters.

Rocks and fossils

Living things are born all the time. They may get old and die naturally, or they may be killed. Nature has ways of dealing with dead bodies – something is always at hand to eat them up. This is why we don't see dead bodies everywhere. But if they escape being eaten, there is a chance that their bones may be preserved in rocks, like the ones you see here. This is Dinosaur National Monument in the USA, a place where the rock layers contain huge numbers of dinosaur bones.

▼ This is one of the most important places for dinosaur bones on Earth. But you wouldn't know it from a casual glance. It is why geologists need to be sharp-eyed. Most of the bones are still buried in the rocks, and you only see them where streams have cut valleys. There the bones stick out from the valley sides.

The discovery of dinosaurs

Fossils are all formed the same way, whether they be dinosaurs, trees or fish. But what made dinosaur fossils so exciting to early scientists was the idea that 'monsters' far bigger than anything alive today, had once walked on Earth.

It is probable that people have seen dinosaur fossils for tens of thousands of years. They may often have walked past an oddly-shaped 'rock' and kicked it to one side.

It took a long time for **FOSSIL** bones to be recognised for what they really were. In 1677 Robert Plot made a step in the right direction when he found a dinosaur bone in a quarry. He thought it might have been from an elephant brought to Britain by the Romans. Then he decided instead that it was the fossil bone of a giant!

In the 18th century people began to take these odd rocks – fossils (picture ②) – seriously and this helped develop the science called geology (although, strictly speaking, people who study fossils are called palaeontologists). They also found strange indentations in some rocks (picture ④) and even some ball-shaped features (picture ③). All were mysteries.

In the 19th century scientists began to recognise these things as fossils and then they started to identify and to classify them. The first fossil to be identified correctly as a dinosaur was named by Oxford University Professor William Buckland in 1824. He called it Megalosaurus (*saurus* means 'lizard', and so Megalosaurus means 'great lizard').

The word dinosaur was coined by another Oxford professor, Sir Richard Owen, in 1842. *Deinos* in Greek means 'terrible'. By terrible, he was referring to its size, not its teeth or claws (picture ①). Incidentally, Owen was one of the scientists who thought the ideas on evolution by Charles Darwin were a lot of rubbish. Whereas, in fact, they would have helped him to explain the dinosaur he had just named!

▲ ① An Acrocanthosaurus fossil skull.

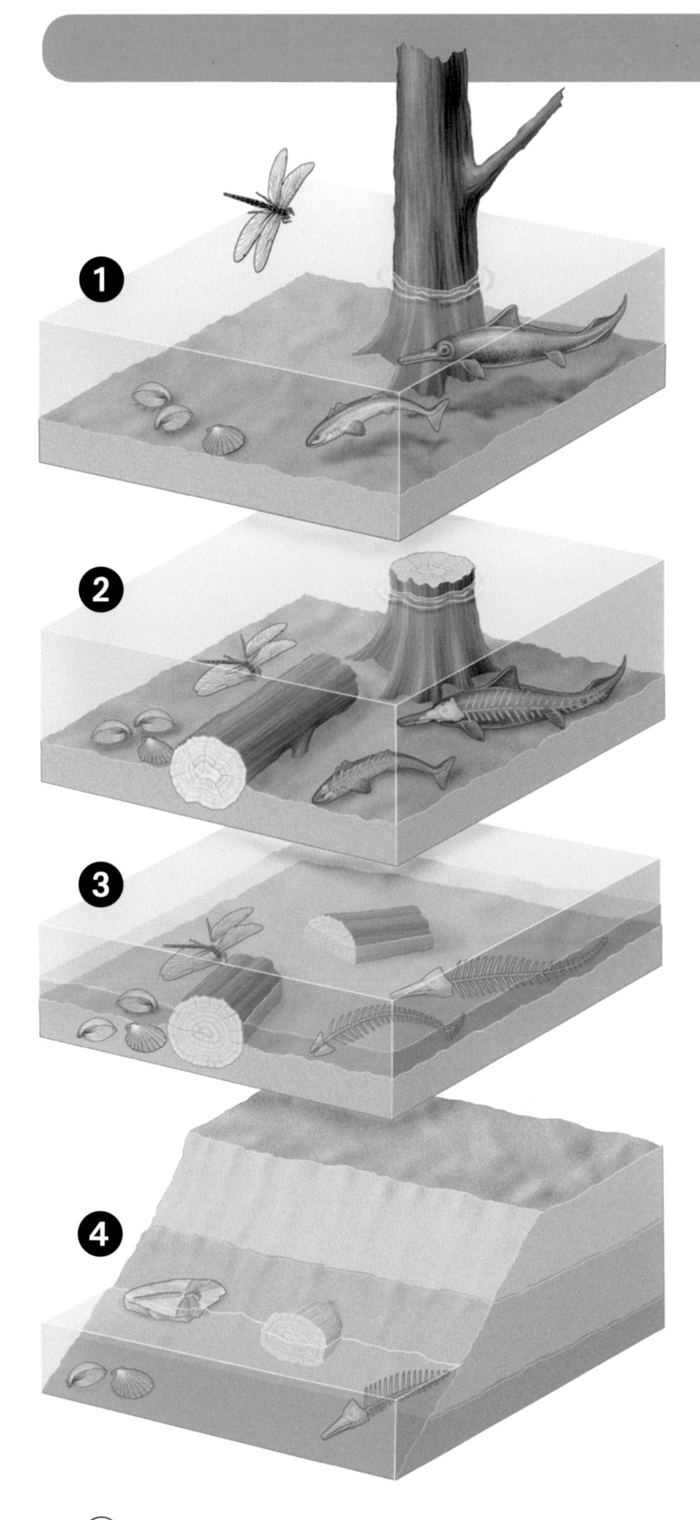

◀ (2) As you know, flesh normally decays very quickly and bones are eaten by scavengers. But under special circumstances the rate of decay can be slowed right down. This happens if animals (or plants) are buried in muds and sands during a flood, for example. If this happens quickly, it gives a chance for something remarkable to happen. It is buried without being eaten or broken up by wind or waves. When the animal or plant eventually decomposes in its rocky tomb, a space is left in the rock showing what shape it was. Furthermore, the bones of the dead animals and the tissues of dead plants are usually changed into new minerals over time. In this way they are changed to 'stone'. They have become fossils.

Rocks that were once buried in this way may come to the surface tens or hundreds of millions of years later when rivers cut into them or the sea cuts into a cliff. Sometimes people cut into rocks by digging quarries.

Many fossil minerals are harder than the rocks they are in. As the rocks wash away, the fossils are temporarily exposed. Of course, once exposed, it is only by chance that the fossil is discovered by scientists. Most are washed away during floods or destroyed by quarrying and never seen again.

This diagram shows the series of events that leads to fossilisation. ❶ A lagoon with animals. ❷ Animals and trees die and begin to decay. ❸ They start to be buried by sand and mud and some of their remains turn into fossils. ❹ The bottom picture shows how the fossils are exposed millions of years later when the rocks are cut into by rivers.

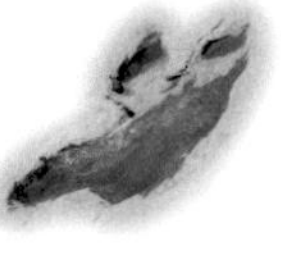

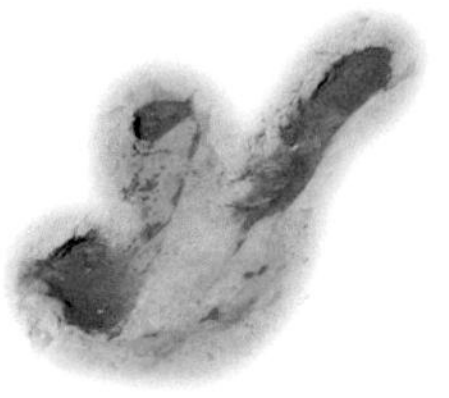

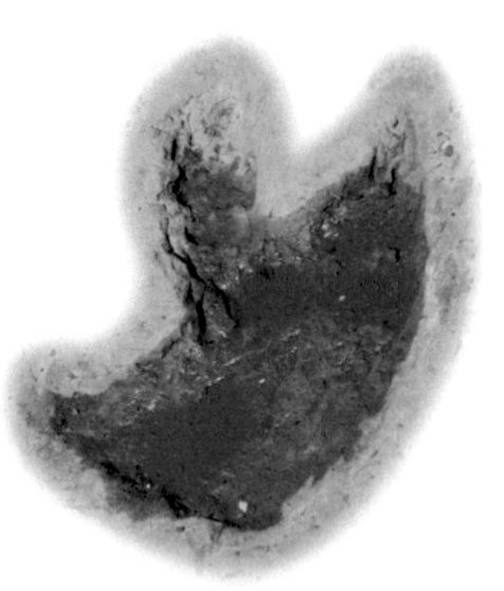

▶ (4) These three-toed, two-legged dinosaur footprints were made by a dinosaur walking over mud. The impression dried out and hardened. A flood came along and filled the impressions with sand or silt and then buried the whole lot in more sand and silt. Gradually it all turned into rock. Now rivers are stripping the rock away and washing the sand and silt out of the footprints, so they look almost as they would have perhaps 150 million years ago.

▼ (3) These are natural casts of a dinosaur foot (probably a two-legged plant-eater) and a piece of dinosaur dung (called a coprolite).

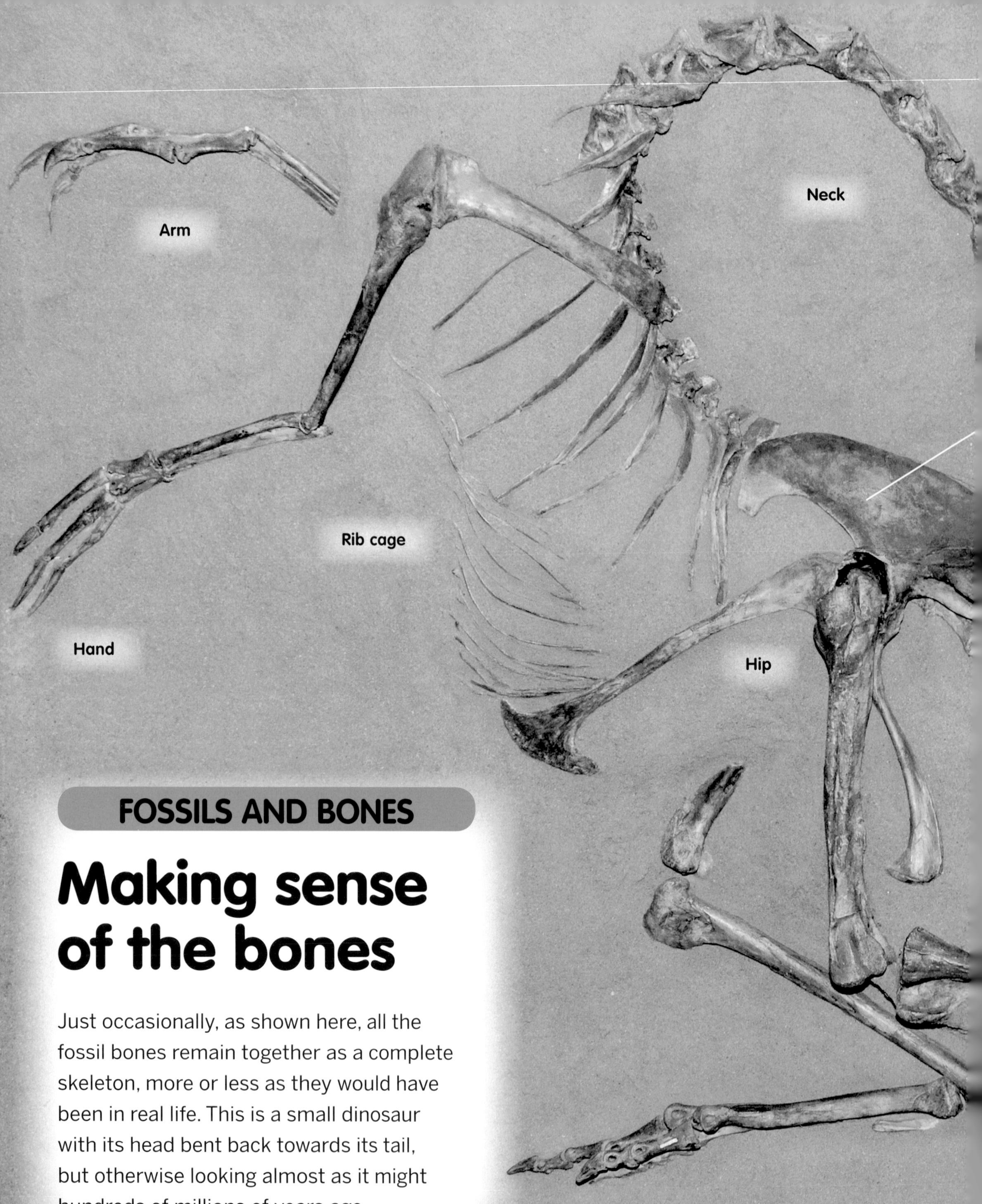

Arm

Neck

Rib cage

Hand

Hip

FOSSILS AND BONES

Making sense of the bones

Just occasionally, as shown here, all the fossil bones remain together as a complete skeleton, more or less as they would have been in real life. This is a small dinosaur with its head bent back towards its tail, but otherwise looking almost as it might hundreds of millions of years ago.

Pelvis

This is the part of our bodies – and of all other land animals – that holds the body together, in a manner of speaking. The pelvis is the big blade-shaped bone. See how the leg bone is attached to it through a huge ball and socket, rather like ours. This is what made it possible for dinosaurs to walk upright – as it does for us. From it comes the backbones (left) and the tail bones (right).

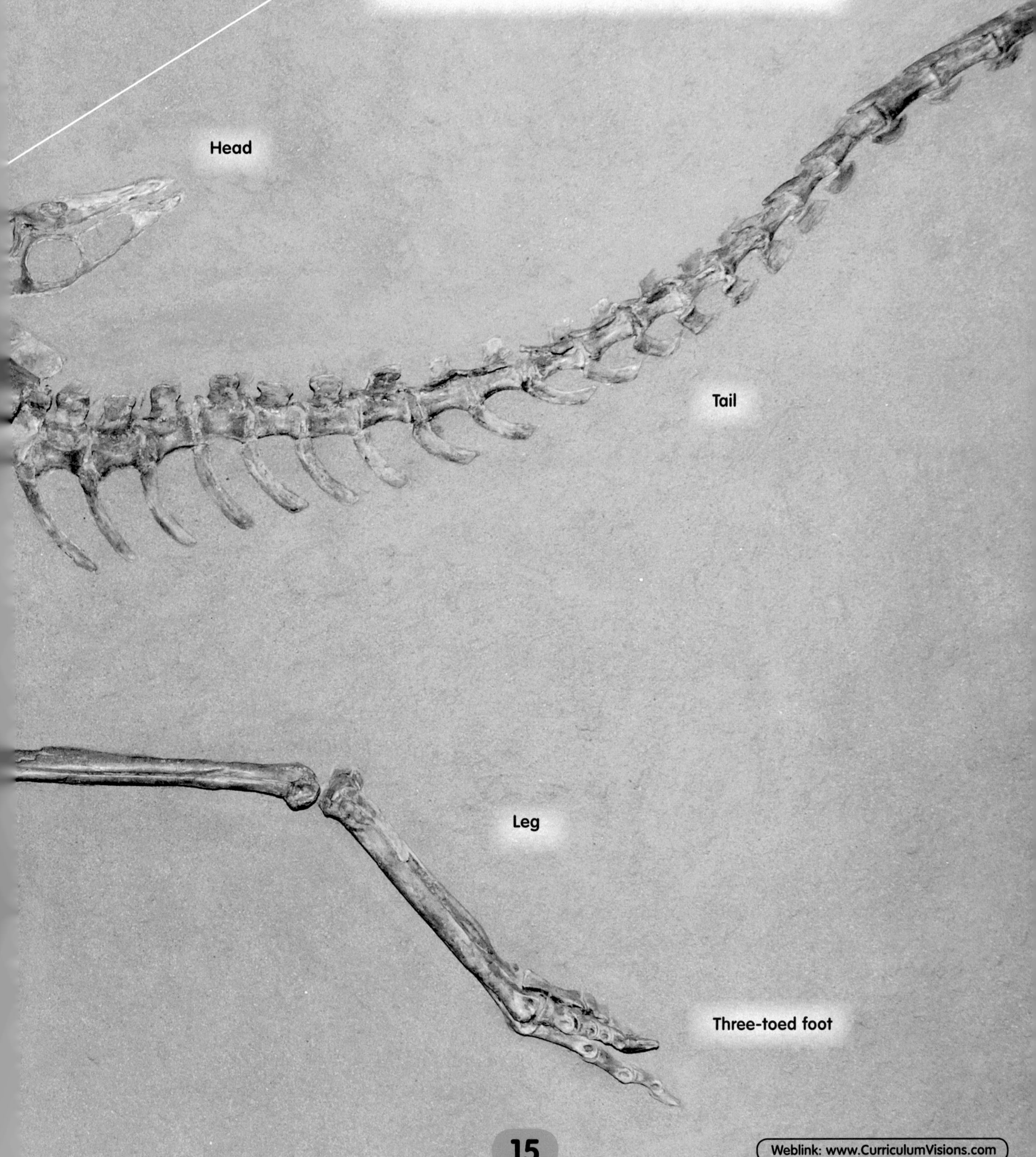

Head

Tail

Leg

Three-toed foot

What we can tell from bones

Bones are a mineral, a kind of stone. It's called calcium phosphate by scientists. In life, bones are living things and have blood vessels and marrow (tissues and fat cells) as well as the hard (mineral) part.

▲ (1) A bone which has survived 100 million years with very little change. The pitted surface shows the holes where the blood vessels used to be when the dinosaur was alive. You can tell a lot about dinosaurs from a sample like this.

◀ (2) This is what you normally find. The shape of the bone is preserved in the rocks, but the bone has been completely replaced by minerals. You can tell very little detail from a specimen like this.

When animals die, the blood stops flowing and the bones stop growing. Bones and teeth of the dinosaurs were pretty hard and already made of minerals, but even so, when they got buried in the ground, they began to change into fossil minerals (scientists call it mineralisation). This occurs on a microscopic scale – for example, the tiny spaces of the original bone where the blood vessels and marrow were, often become filled with new minerals. The original hard parts of the bones and teeth may remain hardly altered, but usually the bone is replaced with new minerals, too (picture (2)).

Not all bones mineralise in the same way. You can get a rough idea of how far they have changed by their weight. If bones are heavy, then the pores have been mostly filled with minerals. If they are light they have been only partly mineralised (picture (1)).

However far the process has gone, and even if the bones still look like bones, they are, strictly speaking, now stones.

Bone 'rings'

Living bones, a bit like tree trunks, record the history of their growth. Like a tree ring, the limb bones show the amount of growth in a given period, and how fast the bone was growing.

By looking at the growth lines in bones we can tell that young dinosaurs grew at incredibly high rates, as fast as or faster than any modern mammal or bird. They became adults in 10 to 20 years.

In general, larger animals grow much faster to their adult size than smaller species do (think elephant). But in dinosaur times there was an especially important advantage to growing. The rush to reach their great adult size, was an advantage because they lived at a time when the land, sea and air was full of hunters of all sizes and shapes that ate anything that moved,

▶ ③ The peg-like tooth of a plant-eating Triceratops.

▶ ④ The dagger-like tooth of a hunting Spinosaurus.

including their own offspring. No matter what your size, something was ready to kill you if it could. So it helped to get to adult size quickly (that is, the dinosaurs who grew quickly were probably more likely to survive and so breed offspring that grew quickly, too. It was an evolutionary advantage).

This is why dinosaurs were not really like large modern reptiles even though they looked somewhat like them. The difference is that dinosaurs grew their bones like birds and mammals, so they grew faster than other reptiles. To do this, they had to have more blood moving through the bones, which is one reason some scientists think they were warm-blooded. In fact, dinosaurs were developing like birds, although they still looked like reptiles 200 million years ago.

What we can tell from skeletons

Most dinosaur skeletons are found incomplete or with their bones scattered. So reconstructing dinosaurs is often a complicated 3D jigsaw exercise. But from the skeleton we can see how big the animal was. By looking at the way its bones are arranged, how heavy they are, and the nature of the joints, we can tell how it moved (picture ⑤) and whether it was a fast runner or a slow one. By looking at its teeth we can tell whether it was mainly a meat-eating hunter (with pointed teeth) (picture ④) or a plant-eater (with peg-shaped or flat grinding teeth) (picture ③).

▼ ⑤ This Stegosaurus skeleton model shows four limbs of about the same size. It must have walked on all fours. Its peg-like teeth tell us it was a plant-eater. Its size allows us to guess its weight. But the plates on the top of its spine are like nothing we see today and so they remain a mystery (although there have been lots of guesses, see page 19).

Adding flesh to the skeleton

Reconstructing what a dinosaur was like means understanding how it lived, what it ate and how it moved. Although we know some things, there are many 'grey areas' where knowledge is uncertain, and quite a few areas where we are still completely in the dark.

The skeleton of a dinosaur gives us a rough idea of its size, but the shape of the soft flesh is much harder to work out (picture ②). Look at the pictures of a skeleton and compare it with a mummy (picture ①) to see how different they are even without muscles.

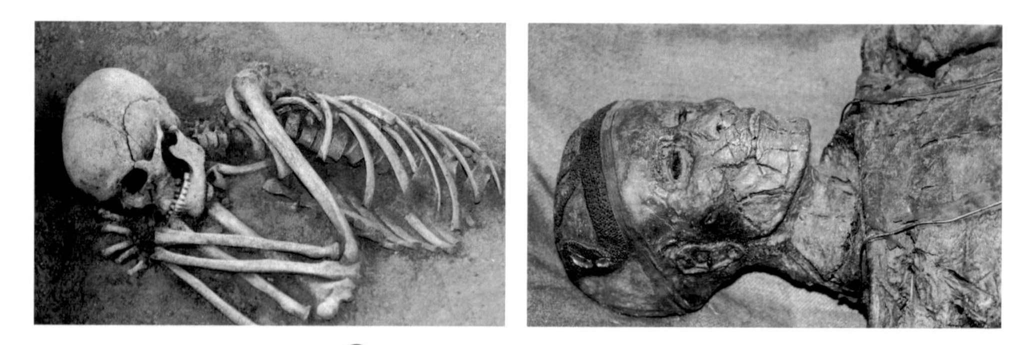

▲ ① When people are buried in the ground much of their flesh soon disappears. Very occasionally, however, special conditions preserve the tissues as well, as in the case of an Egyptian mummy. Notice the difference between the mummy and the skeleton. It is much easier to imagine what the person looked like from looking at the mummy because it still has skin. Very occasionally, dinosaur remains are well preserved, too. When they are, scientists can find out much more about the world of dinosaurs.

The closest relatives to dinosaurs are lizards, so we can look at lizards as a guide (but remember lizards are not very closely related). People see that lizards, for example, use colour as camouflage, for display when attracting a mate and for defence. The patterns seen on lizards are often used for dinosaur reproductions because this is the best comparison we have. However, this has its limits. On the previous page we saw a skeleton of a bus-sized Stegosaurus, a dinosaur from the late **JURASSIC** period

◀ ② Here is an X-ray of a human foot. You can see the bones clearly, but look for the shadow around them, which is the shape of the foot as we would normally see it. The flesh adds a lot of 'padding' to the foot, sometimes in places we would not be able to predict from the bones alone. When people reconstruct dinosaurs from their bones, they have to add lots of padding, but as there are few clues to work with, it is hard to get close to what dinosaurs really looked like.

▲ ③ Kentrosaurus (meaning 'pointed lizard' after the spines) is a relation of Stegosaurus but was just 4 metres long and weighed only 320 kg. It had a double row of plates running halfway down its spine, which then gave way to a single row of spines. It also had spikes on its flanks. It was found in Africa, whereas Stegosaurus was found in North America. The fact that they are so similar helps to confirm that both Africa and North America were once joined (into a continent known as PANGEA) which then drifted apart in the Jurassic. From this time, Kentrosaurus and Stegosaurus developed (evolved) differently.

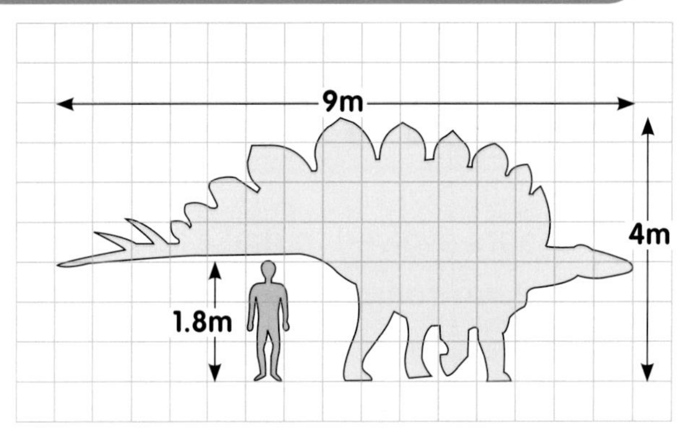

▲▼ ④ Stegosaurus compared to a man.

(155 to 145 million years ago). The name Stegosaurus comes from the Greek for 'roof lizard', named after the very distinctive plates across its back.

It lived at the same time as giants like Diplodocus (page 35) and Apatosaurus (formerly called Brontosaurus, page 34).

No one really knows what the back plates were for, but some people have suggested that they were covered in skin and blood vessels and used to steady the body temperature. Other people think they were for display. It had metre-long spikes on its tail and we can be more confident that they were probably used to flail from side to side to repel any attacks from hunting dinosaurs. Stegosaurus was related to Kentrosaurus (picture ③), but much bigger.

It was a plant-eater with stubby teeth, so it would not have been a particularly ferocious dinosaur. It ate while supported on all fours, although it may well have reached up to browse on its two back legs.

The skeleton on page 17 and the reconstructions on this page let you see how the 'flesh' has been put on the bones (picture ④). Notice that Stegosaurus was probably quite a broad animal, and this is typical of most plant-eaters.

Rulers of the land

Dinosaurs evolved to make use of every kind of natural environment. As a result some were small, some were large, some were plant-eaters and some were hunters of other dinosaurs.

As they evolved, some species died out and others took their place. As a result, dinosaurs that lived at the start of 'dinosaur times' were mostly different species to the ones that lived at the end of 'dinosaur times'.

A matter of survival

Before we look at some of the types of dinosaur, let us just remember one thing: dinosaurs and all other living things had to eat to live. That basic need determined where they lived, how they behaved, and much of what they did.

There is only one kind of living thing that can live without any other and that is the plants. Plants get their energy from sunlight and the materials they need to grow from rain and the soil. Everything else – all animals including dinosaurs – gets its food by eating plants or other animals.

This means that, in the time of the dinosaurs, the amount of plants, what they were like and where they grew, controlled how many dinosaurs there were and where they lived. Some dinosaurs could eat plants (just like elephants), but others could only digest meat (like lions). Meat-eating dinosaurs couldn't eat plants, so they would have died if they had eaten up all of the plant-eating dinosaurs. There had to be a balance. It meant there had to be more plant-eating dinosaurs around than meat-eating dinosaurs. These connections are called a food chain.

▼ (1) Gigantoraptor was a dinosaur that lived 85 million years ago (during the late CRETACEOUS period). It was discovered as recently as 2005 in Inner Mongolia. It was 8 metres long and weighed 1.4 tonnes.

It looked remarkably similar to a bird, having a beak and no teeth. It probably had feathers.

Its huge upper rear legs meant it could move very fast, like a modern emu (it would have left lumbering T. rex far behind).

In general, healthy grown-up plant-eating dinosaurs could see off the hunting dinosaurs, either by herding together, running fast or just being gigantic. Hunters tended to eat the young, the ill and the old. As a result, they may have needed to roam over vast territories just to find enough food. Hunters would also have had to protect these territories, and looking fierce is one way to do this. Hunting dinosaurs looked fierce because they could rear up and show a face full of sharp teeth (picture ②). Plant-eating dinosaurs mostly had armour for protection.

If there are many types of environment, then there is a chance for different types of dinosaur to survive. People have identified over 500 dinosaur groups so far.

Dinosaurs walked differently from other reptiles. Their legs were under their bodies (like us). If their legs had been at the sides (like lizards or crocodiles) they could never have grown to be huge because they could not have supported the weight of their bodies.

Supporting the body like this also meant that dinosaurs could breathe more easily than lizards, they would have had more stamina and could have kept walking or running for long periods. Lizards and crocodiles skuttle, and then only for short distances. This is why they rely on ambushing their prey. Dinosaurs were probably also different inside from lizards, more like half way between a lizard (which is cold-blooded) and a bird (which is warm-blooded) (picture ①).

▼ ② Dilophosaurus means 'two-crested lizard' because it had two boney crests on its head. It was one of the earliest Jurassic meat-eating dinosaurs (theropods, pages 40–49). It was six metres long and weighed half a tonne (see picture ③, page 24).

The crests may have been used for courtship display. The pattern of its teeth would have made it look like the teeth in a crocodile. However, it did not chase prey but was a scavenger, tearing the flesh of dead carcasses. One of its closest relatives was probably Cryolophosaurus (pages 48–49).

Food

The plant-eaters mainly ate coniferous trees and ferns (grass did not exist at this time). Early plant-eating dinosaurs didn't have crushing teeth, so they would have had to use their teeth to strip the leaves from plants and then swallow them whole. Their teeth were often peg-like as a result. To help break up food, plant-eaters swallowed stones which moved around with the food in their stomachs, helping to shred it and release the nourishment.

▲ ③ **Triceratops defending itself from Dilophosaurus using its bulk and huge bony head.**

Dinosaur size

Dinosaurs reached gigantic sizes early in their evolution. Large plant-eating animals are often more efficient in digesting food than small ones. Since larger animals have longer digestive systems, food is digested for much longer, which means they could have survived on poorly nutritious plants. This is because, the longer the gut, the more time microbes have to ferment plant material, and so help digestion.

Even when parts of the world were more lush, many dinosaurs still lived in places which nowadays we call tropical savanna. It's the same sort of place that elephants live in today, suggesting that poor-quality food in dry environments is best suited to giant plant-eaters.

Dinosaurs varied in size from a turkey (Microraptor was less than 0.6 m long) to a house and more. But, in general, they tended to be on the large size and, of course, some were gigantic. So, for example, prehistoric mammoths, which were bigger than modern elephants, would have been dwarfed by the giant plant-eaters (**SAUROPODS**), and in the oceans only the biggest whales could have rivalled the pterosaurs in size.

Giant plant-eaters

The tallest and heaviest dinosaur known from good skeletons is a Brachiosaurus: 12 metres tall and 22.5 metres long, weighing up to 60 tonnes. The longest complete dinosaur skeleton is the 27 m long Diplodocus.

Although these were immense, there are some bones that suggest that there were even larger dinosaurs. Argentinosaurus may have weighed 100 tonnes; Sauroposeidon

▶ (4) **Suchomimus was a hunting dinosaur with a very long crocodile-like snout. It lived in Africa in the Cretaceous 125 to 112 million years ago. It may have been a fish eater. It was up to 12 m long. It was related to Spinosaurus.**

Living together

If you were a plant-eater, you may have needed to be wary of the hunters, not just for yourself but also for your young. Being in a herd helped. We know that plant-eating dinosaurs often did this because fossil beds contain the remains or the fossil footprints of many plant-eating dinosaurs.

may have been 18 m tall. Amphicoelias may even have weighed over 120 tonnes, but as we have few bones of them this can only be guesswork.

Hunting giants

Hunters would not have got the same advantages from being gigantic. Nevertheless, even though most hunting dinosaurs were not as gigantic as the big plant-eaters, an average hunting dinosaur was ten times the weight of a large hunting animal such as a bear today (picture (4)).

The largest known hunting dinosaur was Spinosaurus, which reached a length of 18 metres and weighed 8 tonnes. It was bigger than Tyrannosaurus rex.

If you were a hunter and very large, it may have been better to hunt alone (just as bears do today). But if you were smaller, like Dilophosaurus (picture (2), page 23, and picture (3), page 24) or younger, it may have been better to work in packs, such as the wild dogs do today.

▶ (5) HADROSAURS, or duck-billed, crested dinosaurs, were descended from Iguanodons. They had two long back legs, but probably also walked on all fours. They were plant-eaters. This is the skeleton of a duck-billed Lambeosaurus, a small hadrosaur. You can see the crest on its head very well. Its mouth looked like that of a duck and it used its beak for cropping plants. Food was sent to the back of the mouth into cheek pouches and ground up using thousands of teeth.

Frills and fancies

One of the most striking things about many dinosaurs are their frills, crests (pictures (5) and (6)) and huge spinal plates (page 19). But modern lizards have frills and crests, too, and they use them when they are courting and also when they are trying to protect their territory from others. It is possible that this is what dinosaurs used their frills and crests for, although no-one knows for sure.

▼ (6) Saurolophus (which means 'lizard crest') belongs to the group of large plant-eating duck-billed hadrosaurs that lived close to the end of dinosaur times. It had a spike-like crest which stuck out from the back of its skull. It was about 10 m long and weighed 2 tonnes.

Dinosaur eggs and young

Many creatures lay eggs, from turtles to birds to crocodiles. Dinosaurs are related to all of these.

Some dinosaurs laid eggs in groups, like turtles. Others dug many pits and laid an egg in each one. In both cases, this tells us that dinosaurs took a lot of care over their eggs, so we might expect that they remained with the nest to guard the eggs, too.

Most dinosaur eggs hatched, or were dug up and eaten by other dinosaurs, so there are few fossil eggs or nests. But in a few cases they have been left undisturbed because they were buried by floods or other events. Once buried, water seeped through the pores in the shell (which are needed in all shells to allow the baby to breathe) and then minerals dissolved in the water formed inside the eggs.

The shell is little changed by this process as it is already a mineral. The inside is rarely preserved.

Dinosaur eggs were big, but they were not enormous. The bigger the egg, the thicker its shell needed to be in order not to break due to the weight of the baby inside. But if the shell was too thick the baby would never be able to break it and hatch. This is what limited the size of dinosaur eggs. Sauropods laid the biggest eggs – they were round and up to 18 cm long and with shells up to 5 mm thick. The egg inside would have been 5 litres! Theropod eggs are mostly 10-15 cm long, oval, and a couple of millimetres thick.

Those young that did survive would have grown very quickly. In the case of giant dinosaurs they may have put on a kilo or so a day and perhaps a tonne a year. Even so, they would have had to keep out of the way of adult hunters (even if they were growing up to be hunters themselves) and so probably lived in the shelter of forests until they were strong enough to be able to defend themselves on the more open plains.

Gigantic plant-eaters

There were two kinds of giant plant-eating dinosaurs: those that walked on two legs (mainly called ornithopods – bird feet) and those that walked on all fours (and called **SAUROPODS**). You can see a two-legged plant-eater on this page. Sauropods were the biggest of all dinosaurs and the largest animals ever to have lived on land. Famous sauropods included Diplodocus, Apatosaurus (which used to be called Brontosaurus) and Brachiosaurus. Sauropods could not chew and had to swallow rocks to grind their food. Ornithopods had chewing teeth.

▶ Plateosaurus ('flat lizard') was a plant-eating dinosaur belonging to the Triassic. It lived in Europe 215 to 200 million years ago. It had a small head with a long neck and plant-crushing teeth. Plateosaurus was one of the earliest and largest dinosaurs to be discovered. It was 10 m long and weighed three quarters of a tonne. Its eyes were on the sides of its head. Its all-round vision allowed it to keep a watch for hunters. Plateosaurus had 'arms' which were much shorter than the 'legs' and each 'hand' had 'fingers' and a spiked 'thumb'.

What sauropods were like

Sauropods all have long necks and long tails. The tails and neck balanced each other like a giant seesaw. The largest sauropods were bigger than a bus.

Scientists separate dinosaurs into two groups based on the shape of their skeletons. The most common group had hips similar to modern lizards and these included both the plant-eaters (called sauropods) and meat-eaters (called **THEROPODS**). The other group had hips similar to modern birds and include ornithopods. However, for most people, shape and pattern of life are also what matter. The sauropods (meaning 'lizard foot') are what people think of as the classic long-necked, plant-eaters.

Sauropods

Sauropods are among the oldest dinosaurs and they appeared in Triassic time. They were very successful and were common throughout the world in Jurassic times. Some of the most common are Apatosaurus (previously called Brontosaurus), Brachiosaurus (picture ②, page 32) and Diplodocus. You may very well find a skeleton of one of these giants in a museum, but it is unlikely it will be complete because they were simply too big to allow all of the skeleton to remain in place.

Sauropods are not as easy to tell apart as other dinosaurs. They all had small heads,

▼ ① A reconstruction of sauropods in the forest edge. Trees show their gigantic size.

long necks, great barrel bodies and long balancing tails. The tails of some were quite thin and may have been used in defence. You would not want to receive a whiplash from a 20 m-long tail.

Some probably stood on their hind legs, at least for part of the time. Many were able to arch their necks up high, while others, like Diplodocus, probably could not. We can tell the difference by looking at the neck bones. Some can be bent more than others. In general, sauropods kept their heads level with their body. Sauroposeidon, however, could crane its neck and might have been able to reach up to 18 metres (four times as tall as a giraffe), and if it were alive today could easily have looked in at a third-storey window.

On the other hand, if some were alive today, they would need the roads reinforced. Argentinosaurus weighed up to 100 tonnes and Bruhathkayosaurus may have weighed 200 tonnes. (For comparison, an elephant weighs 10 tonnes.) From tip to toe, Supersaurus was 40 m long and Amphicoelias (the world's longest ever animal) may have been 60 metres long (see page 33). Even the smallest were 6 m long.

Sauropods had teeth for chewing tough plants and must have had a giant stomach for digesting them. They laid eggs and had feet with five toes. Some had plates which have mostly been thought of as armour plates.

Animals of the plains

Because sauropods were mostly huge, they could not get in the forests, but had to browse on the ferns that grew on the plains. The reconstruction in picture (1) gives you an idea of their immense scale. Nonetheless, the forests may well have been important to their young, who kept out of

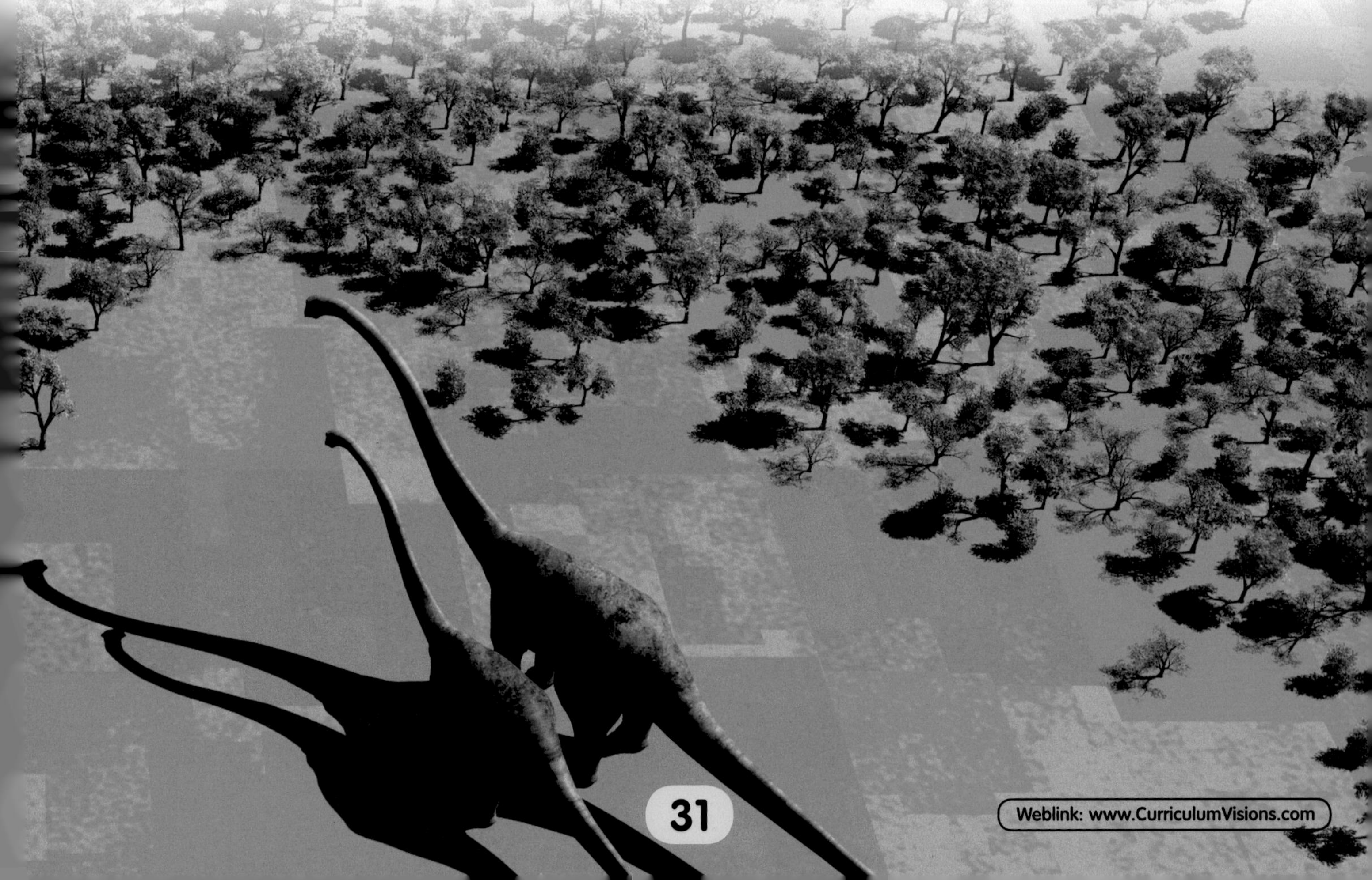

the way of hunting dinosaurs among the trees until they were big enough to look after themselves.

Brachiosaurus

Brachiosaurus (which means 'arm lizard') was a sauropod with front limbs longer than the back, so it sloped back towards its rump, something like a giraffe does (pictures (2) and (4)). The first toe on the front arms of a Brachiosaurus and the first three toes on its hind feet had claws.

Brachiosaurus was 25 metres long and the top of its head would have reached 13 metres or more above the ground. It probably weighed about 30 tonnes.

Brachiosaurus must have been an amazing eater. Just to keep itself alive it would have had to eat about 200 kg of food a day (equal to 25 sacks of potatoes).

Brachiosauruses were just too big to have been attacked by any hunting dinosaur.

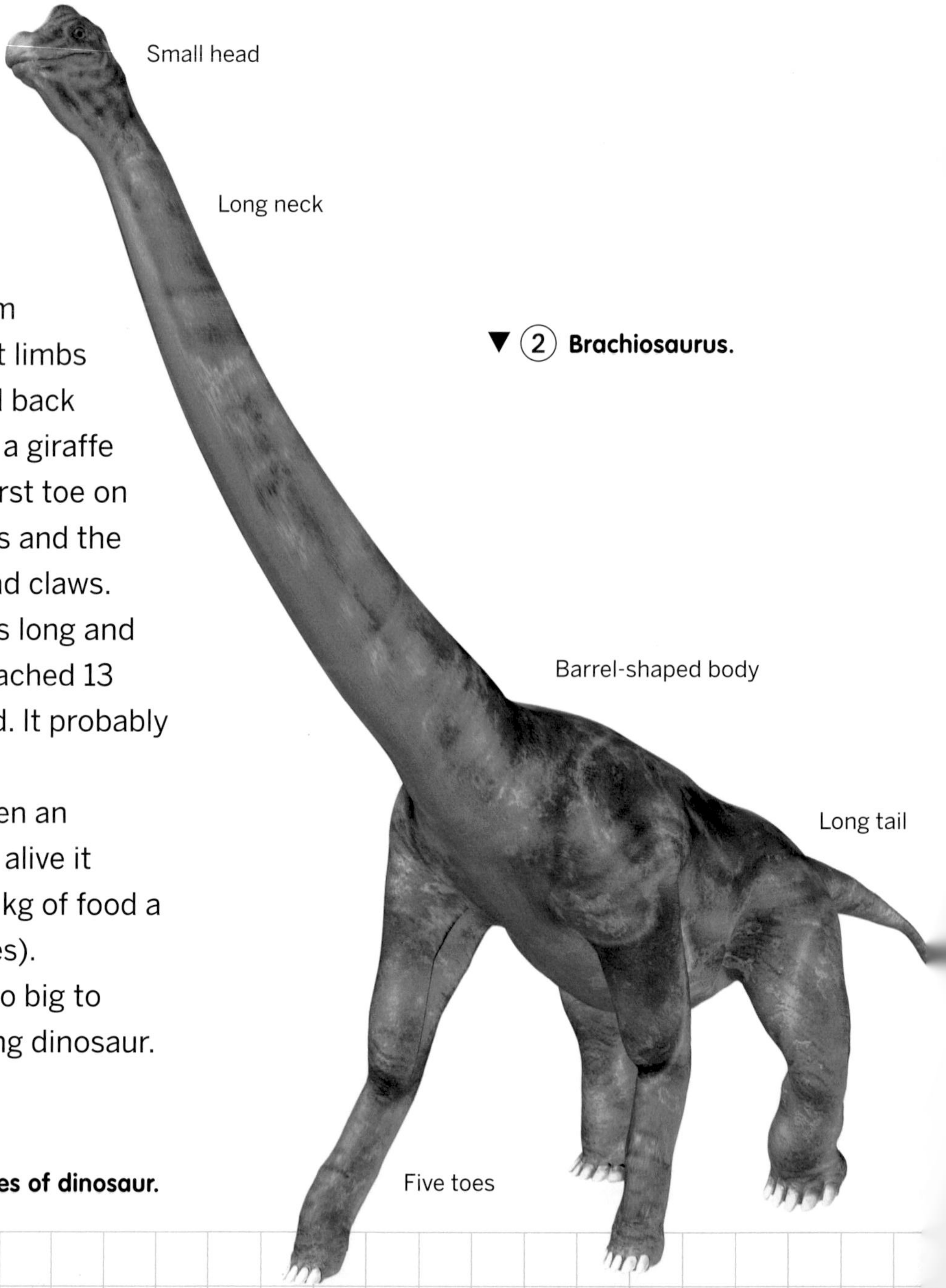

▼ (2) **Brachiosaurus.**

▼ (3) **Size comparisons of different types of dinosaur.**

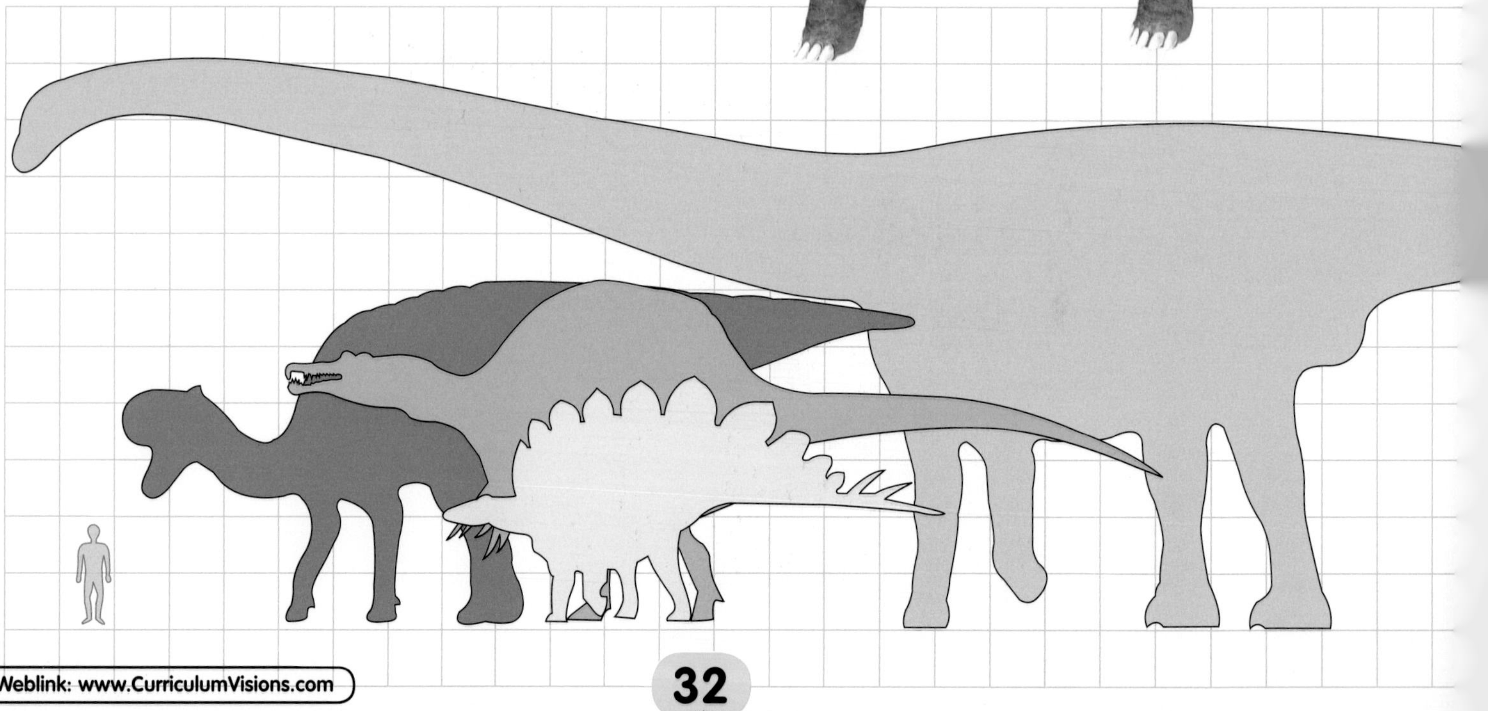

Amphicoelias

Amphicoelias may have been one of the world's largest dinosaurs (pictures (3) and (5)). Only a hip bone and a leg bone have ever been found, so the whole dinosaur was reconstructed from just two bones. As these bones were large versions of what most Diplodocus bones look like, Amphicoelias has been reconstructed in much the same shape. It may have been up to 60 metres long.

▲ (4) **Brachiosaurus**

◀ (5) **Amphicoelias.**

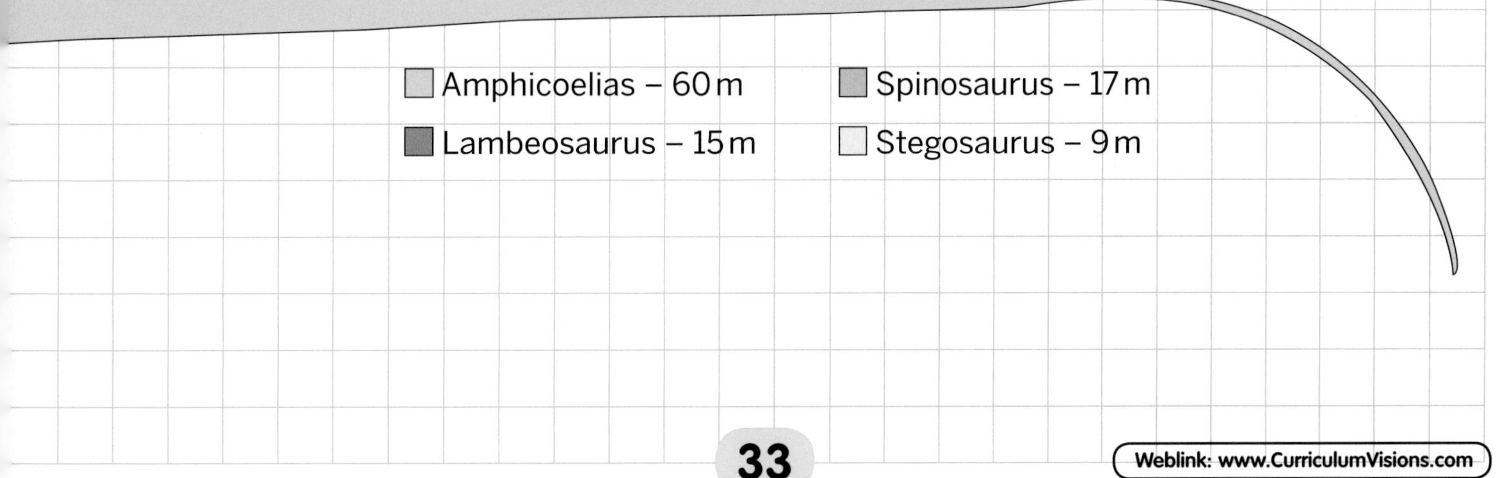

Apatosaurus (Brontosaurus)

(Originally called Apatosaurus (meaning 'deceptive lizard'), it became known as Brontosaurus for decades, but scientists have now gone back to its original name.)

This is perhaps the best known Jurassic sauropod. It was over 20 m long and weighed up to 25 tonnes.

Apatosaurus was a tough guy. It was more heavily built than its other large relatives such as Diplodocus. Yet it had quite a thin, almost delicate-looking tail. This was so mobile it could easily have been flicked like a whip and anything that got in the way would surely have known about it.

Apatosaurus has often been shown with its neck and head held high in the air (picture ⑥), but scientists have examined the neck bones and now believe this was unlikely and that the animal kept its head bent down. If its head had been too high for too long, its heart would have had trouble pumping blood to its brain!

Although it was toughly built, the vast bodyweight, as with other sauropods, meant that, most likely, once it grew up it could never lie down, for its

◀ ⑥ **Apatosaurus**

legs would not have the strength to get it off the ground again. So it probably locked its legs and went to sleep standing up.

Its lungs moved huge volumes of air in and out with each breath. This is an important finding, for, if Apatosaurus had been a true reptile its lungs would have been much smaller – reptiles don't breathe as much as most other animals. Instead its lung space was more like the kind of space (scaled up) that birds have. With a bird-like lung system, it would have been able to walk long distances and even break out into a long-distance run, something that reptiles cannot do.

Diplodocus

Diplodocus (pronounced DI-plod-oh-kuss) lived in North America (picture ⑦). By the end of the Jurassic, when Diplodocus ranged over the land, America had already split away from Europe and Africa due to **CONTINENTAL DRIFT**. It lived with its related sauropods, such as Apatosaurus.

It had many of the same characteristics as Apatosaurus, such as four stump-like legs and a whip-like tail, but it was much more slender and not so barrel shaped. Its limbs were about the same size, so its body was largely held horizontal. The biggest may have been over 50 m long and weighed over 50 tonnes.

Diplodocus was different to other sauropods: it probably used its teeth to strip leaves from branches. By propping itself on its back legs and using its tail as a kind of tripod, it could have reached very high, perhaps stripping leaves as high as 10 m above the ground.

Diplodocus chewed nothing, all the food slipped down into the stomach where it rolled around with stones that the Diplodocus swallowed for the purpose of grinding the food and releasing nourishment. Of course, what goes in must come out, and Diplodocus dropped a tonne of dung a day, some of which is preserved as fossils called coprolites.

Diplodocus lived for 10 million years. It then became extinct and its place in nature taken over by the **TITANOSAURS** during the **CRETACEOUS**.

▼ ⑦ **Diplodocus.**

Frilled plant-eaters

In the later stages of dinosaur times, a group of plant-eating dinosaurs developed with beaks and huge bony frills behind their heads. They eventually became the most common dinosaur on the planet.

They grew to 9 m long and nearly 6 tonnes in weight. These monsters included Zuniceratops (picture ①), Nedoceratops and Triceratops (picture ④, page 39).

▲ (1) Zuniceratops was a descendant of Protoceratops and an ancestor of Triceratops.

▶ (2) Protoceratops

The group which frilled dinosaurs belong to is **CERATOPSIA**, meaning 'horned faces' (pictures (5) and (6)). They evolved and became very common in Cretaceous times. Triceratops bones make up about 80% of all dinosaur remains from the end of dinosaur times.

Most ceratopsians have a true bone protruding from the top of the jaw (it is not really a fibre horn like a rhinoceros), and a parrot-like beak. The bones of the top of the skull developed into two further 'horns' and a huge frill, sometimes solid, as in the case of Triceratops, more often with holes in, as with Torosaurus, Zuniceratops and Nedoceratops (previously called Diceratops).

They were herding animals, defending themselves from hunters like T. rex by running fast (at about 50 kilometres an hour) and staying together. Nevertheless, their huge numbers meant that the young, old and infirm were a major source of food for the hunting dinosaurs.

As they moved about over the plains, they must have chewed everything in sight, rather like herding animals do today. Their beaks would have made it possible for them to eat the harder, less nutritious plants of Cretaceous times.

▼ (3) Protoceratops from an egg.

Protoceratops

Protoceratops was not large by dinosaur standards, being 60 cm high at the hip and a mere 2 m long (pictures (2) and (3)). This early plant-eater did not have the horns that its descendants developed. Even so it had a jaw packed with dozens of teeth.

Zuniceratops

Zuniceratops was only discovered in 1996. It lived about 10 million years before Triceratops, and had some features that still resemble Protoceratops (picture (1), pages 36–37). It was bigger than Protoceratops,

being 1 m or so tall at the hip and just under 4 m long. It weighed 150 kilos. The bone of its frill is pierced with holes, which would have reduced its weight. It did not have a large central 'horn'.

▼ (4) The skull of a Triceratops.

Triceratops

Triceratops is the most commonly recognised frilled dinosaur. It was the only one with a solid frill (picture (4)).

Triceratops lived in North America right at the end of the time of the dinosaurs, in late Cretaceous times, about 68 million years ago. It is easily recognised because of its bony frill at the back of its skull and for the two large horns on the top of its head, and a smaller horn on its snout. Its jaws held an amazing 800 teeth. It had enough armour to protect itself, and it is likely that hunting dinosaurs only managed to kill the young, old or infirm animals.

The horns may have been useful to fend off attack, but they probably were also used by males to challenge one another in the mating season, much like the way stags use their antlers.

Triceratops grew to 9 m long. It was 3 m tall and weighed up to about 12 tonnes. A quarter of its body length was taken up by its head.

▲ (5) Einiosaurus was a medium-sized 'short-frilled' dinosaur (as opposed to Triceratops, which was a long-frilled dinosaur). Einiosaurus grew to 6 m long.

▲ (6) Styracosaurus means 'spiked lizard' because of the spikes that stood out from its snout and the bony frill around its neck.

Hunting dinosaurs

Tyrannosaurus rex (T. rex), the best known of all dinosaurs, was a hunting dinosaur. It belonged to the group of hunting or scavenging, meat-eating dinosaurs called **THEROPODS**. The name theropod comes from the Greek for 'beast-feet'.

Hunting (meat-eating) dinosaurs first evolved in the Triassic period 220 million years ago and outlasted all other dinosaur groups, although they were never as common as plant-eaters. They were only finally made extinct 65 million years ago. But even then their relatives didn't die out completely but evolved. They are the birds. All theropods had many of the same features as birds: a three-toed foot, a wishbone, and air-filled bones, meaning that their bones weighed less than they appeared.

▶ Tyrannosaurus rex, rearing up on its hind legs to attack. For most of the time, however, it probably held its body more horizontal, as shown on the following pages. It had a stiff tail which could not be whipped in the way that sauropod tails could.

What theropods were like

Theropods were very varied, but they nearly all had pointed teeth designed to gnaw great chunks of flesh from their prey.

The hunting dinosaurs mainly belonged to a group called the theropods. They lived throughout dinosaur times and include the last hunting dinosaur, Tyrannosaurus rex (or T. rex). Theropods continued after the age of dinosaurs, however – and we now call them birds. Most walked on two hind limbs (legs) as these were much bigger than their front limbs (arms). But this did not mean that they walked upright. In fact, except when attacking, they probably kept their heads level with their tails.

The earliest theropod was called Eoraptor, but that soon evolved, and by mid-Jurassic times there were many different kinds of theropod from Tyrannosaurus, to bird-like dinosaurs such as Velociraptor and Archaeopteryx.

Among the theropods, some are famous for their size. Tyrannosaurus was the first one of these giants to be discovered and that is why everyone knows about it. And although it was the most common hunting dinosaur at the end of dinosaur times, it only existed for a fairly short time and it was not even the largest theropod to have lived. Spinosaurus, for example (picture ①), was much longer and heavier.

For a long time, people imagined that these hunters moved fast and caught their prey out on the plains, like a lion catching an antelope. However, we now know that hunting dinosaurs could not run as fast as was once thought. This leads us to think that

▶ ① Spinosaurus was the main fearsome dinosaur modelled in the film *Jurassic Park III.* It was also shown with T. rex, but these animals never lived on the same continent and lived millions of years apart, so this was creative licence by the writers.

the hunters probably laid in ambush for their prey, or ate slow-moving older or infirm prey. They would also have been scavengers of dead dinosaurs.

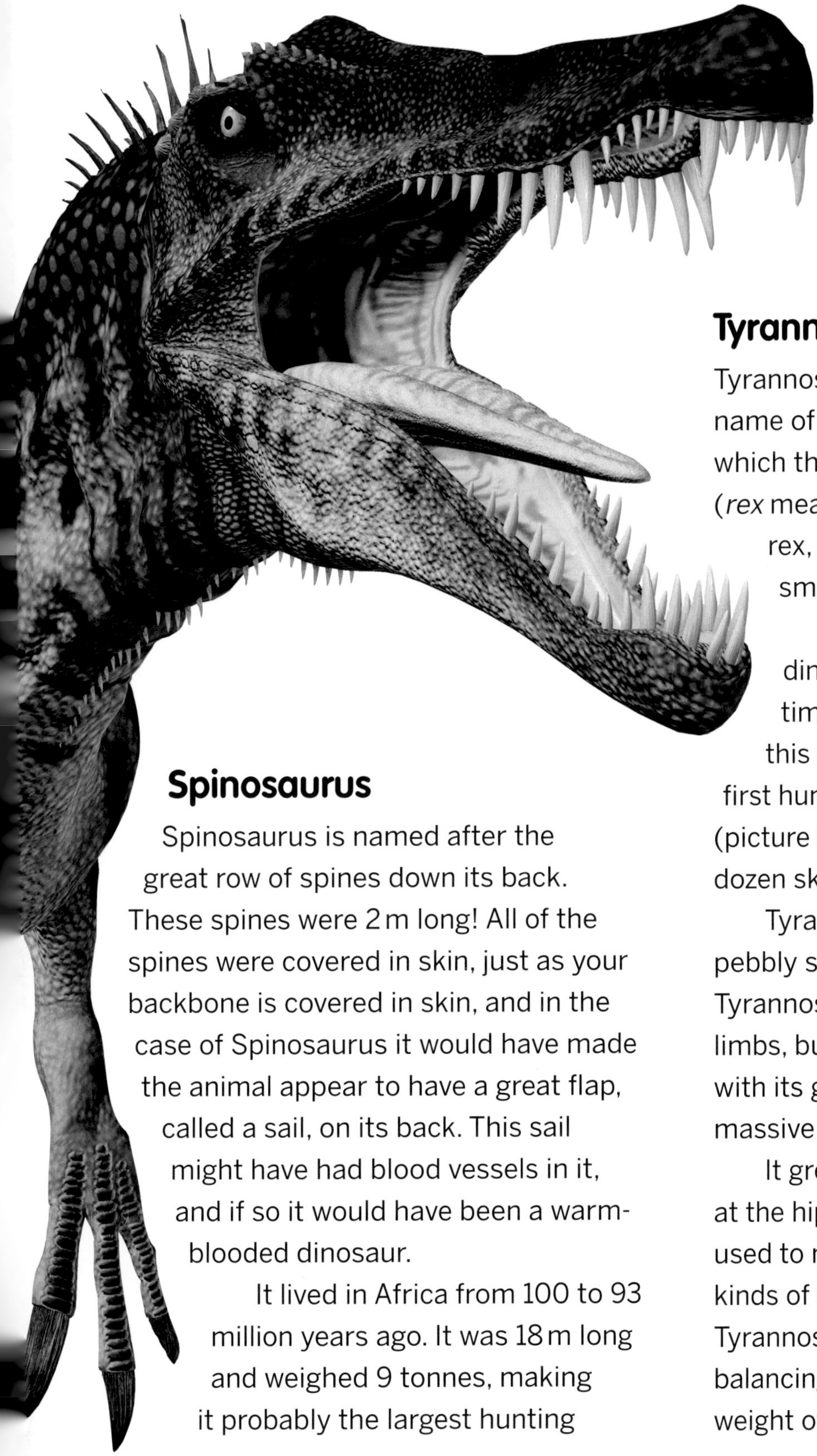

Spinosaurus

Spinosaurus is named after the great row of spines down its back. These spines were 2 m long! All of the spines were covered in skin, just as your backbone is covered in skin, and in the case of Spinosaurus it would have made the animal appear to have a great flap, called a sail, on its back. This sail might have had blood vessels in it, and if so it would have been a warm-blooded dinosaur.

It lived in Africa from 100 to 93 million years ago. It was 18 m long and weighed 9 tonnes, making it probably the largest hunting dinosaur that ever lived. It had one of the longest skulls – about 2 m – of any hunting dinosaur. The skull had a narrow snout filled with straight conical teeth, as you can see in the illustration.

It may well have been a fishing dinosaur because its nostrils were high up on its nose (compare this to a crocodile), but again, like a crocodile, it would have eaten anything that came within reach.

Tyrannosaurus

Tyrannosaurus means 'tyrant lizard'. It is the name of a group (genus) or related species of which the most famous is Tyrannosaurus rex (*rex* means 'king'). The shortened version, T. rex, is often used (note it is capital T, dot, small rex, not T-Rex or other spellings).

Tyrannosaurus was a large hunting dinosaur that lived at the end of dinosaur times (68 to 65 million years ago), and this is probably why its bones were the first hunting dinosaur bones to be discovered (picture ②, pages 44–45). Even so, only a few dozen skeletons have ever been found.

Tyrannosaurus was covered with the pebbly scales common in most dinosaurs. Tyrannosaurus had two 'fingers' on its front limbs, but these limbs were tiny compared with its gigantic rear limbs. It also had a massive head.

It grew up to 13 m long and was 4 m tall at the hips (note that hip measurements are used to make it easier to compare different kinds of dinosaur). Like all dinosaurs, Tyrannosaurus pivoted around its hips, balancing the weight of its head with the weight of its tail. It weighed about 7 tonnes.

▶ (2) This is the head of Tyrannosaurus rex (T. rex) still partly buried in the rocks in which it was found. Notice its great peg-like teeth which curve slightly back.

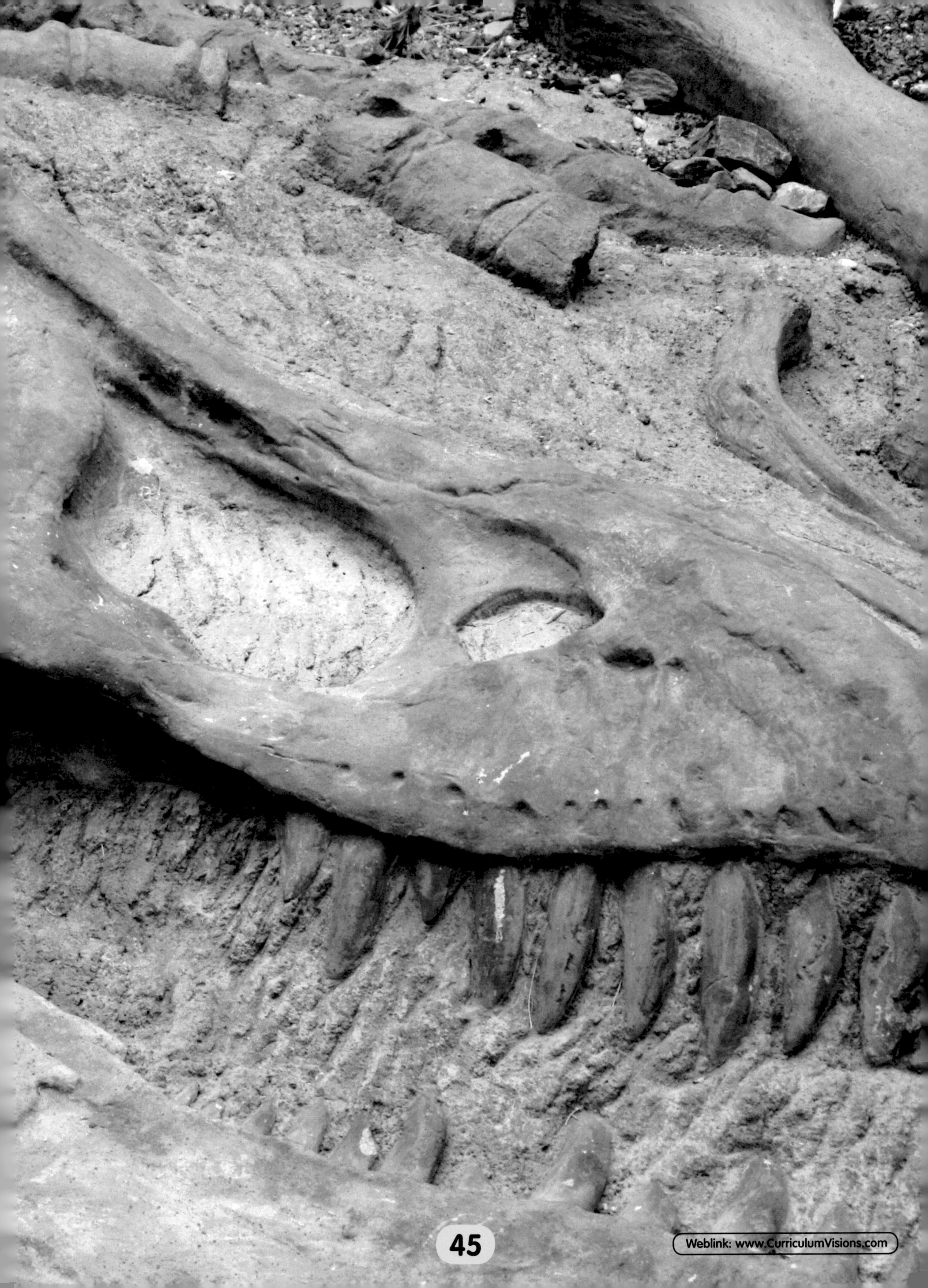

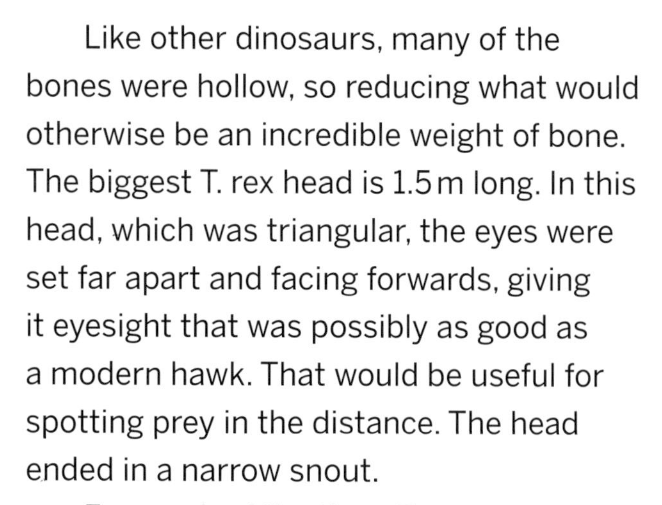

Like other dinosaurs, many of the bones were hollow, so reducing what would otherwise be an incredible weight of bone. The biggest T. rex head is 1.5 m long. In this head, which was triangular, the eyes were set far apart and facing forwards, giving it eyesight that was possibly as good as a modern hawk. That would be useful for spotting prey in the distance. The head ended in a narrow snout.

For much of the time, Tyrannosaurus may also have been a successful scavenger, as it had a very sensitive nose able to smell rotting carcasses from a long way off.

Tyrannosaurus may have been able to run when it was young, but as it grew up this would have become more and more difficult (picture ③). Elephants have the same problem. But although they didn't run, they 'walked' fast and may have reached 40 km an hour. If so, they would have been the fastest large dinosaurs – much faster than their plant-eating prey.

▲ ③ **Tyrannosaurus rex set in front of the forest edge. It is doubtful if a fully-grown animal could have moved through the forests, although the younger animals probably lived among the trees for protection.**

T. rex could bite more powerfully than any other dinosaur. The backward-sloping teeth stopped any prey from slipping away.

T. rex grew 'slowly' at first, still being less than 2 tonnes at the age of 14. Then it put on a phenomenal spurt of growth, adding 600 kg a year for the next four years, before slowing down as it reached adulthood.

Many T. rex seem to have died about 6 years after becoming fully grown, so the animal may not have had a long natural life.

Tarbosaurus (picture ⑧, page 49) is closely related to Tyrannosaurus, but lived and evolved in Mongolia after North America split away from Asia.

Other hunters

There were many other hunters, most of which lived before Tyrannosaurus. Allosaurus, for example, was a common Jurassic hunter. Allosaurus (meaning 'strange lizard', partly because of the double crest on its head) was a large dinosaur that lived 155 to 145 million years ago. It probably grew to 12 m long and was about 10 m tall.

Allosaurus had a gigantic skull, huge hind limbs and tiny forelimbs. Its inner ear was like that of a crocodile, so it probably made, and heard, low sounds. It had a good sense of smell, well suited for tracking down dead animals.

Allosaurus ate large plant-eating dinosaurs such as Stegosaurus, attacking them with its huge jaws filled with rows of sharp teeth. It lived for up to 30 years, quite similar to other large hunters.

Young Allosaurus were much more agile than adults, and probably hunted in packs.

But, as they became older, heavier and slower, they may have become more solitary, protecting their own territory from other Allosauruses (picture ⑤) and settling down to ambushing prey instead of chasing it, or simply scavenging the carcasses of other animals they happened to chance by.

Monolophosaurus (which means 'one-crested lizard') was also a hunter from the Jurassic (picture ④). The first remains were found in 1984. It could grow to be 5 m long, 2 m high and weighed the best part of a tonne. Monolophosaurus is thought to be related to Allosaurus.

Cryolophosaurus means 'cold crest lizard'. It was 6 to 8 metres long. It lived in the early Jurassic period and had a huge crest which ran across, not along, the head above the eyes, fanning out and furrowed to make it look like a comb (picture ⑦). Because it resembled rock-and-roll singer Elvis Presley's haircut, this dinosaur got

▶ ④ **Monolophosaurus**

▼ ⑤ **Allosaurus.**

the nickname 'Elvisaurus' when it was first discovered in 1991.

Cryolophosaurus is the only dinosaur to have been found in Antarctica. It was found with fossilised tree trunks, telling us that Antarctica used to be much warmer (and closer to the Equator) than it is today. Since the Jurassic, Antarctica has moved to the South Pole. Movements of the continents are one of the most important events in the history of the world.

Ceratosaurus means 'horned lizard' because it had a bony horn on its snout and a pair of bony projections over the eyes (picture ⑥). It lived in the Jurassic period. Ceratosaurus was smaller but somewhat similar to Allosaurus being 8 m long, under 3 m at the hip and weighing just a tonne. It survived competition from Allosaurus because its flexible body allowed it to swim and so it got its food by hunting in rivers.

▲ ⑥ **Ceratosaurus**

▼ ⑦ **Cryolophosaurus**

▲ ⑧ **Tarbosaurus**

Fishers of the deep

Marine reptiles were not dinosaurs, but they lived and died at the same time and they were equally spectacular (picture ①).

Ichthyosaur is Greek for 'fish lizard'. For tens of millions of years ichthyosaurs were the masters of the oceans. Then they became extinct and their place was taken by the plesiosaurs.

◀ ① Elasmosaurus.

Ichthyosaurs

Ichthyosaurs were the first giant marine reptiles. Their shape may remind you of a fish and a dolphin, although they are in no way related. The earliest remains are found preserved in Triassic rocks and they did not become extinct until the Cretaceous period.

No one yet knows what the ancestor of an ichthyosaur looked like, but it may have been an early lizard that took to living permanently in the oceans.

Ichthyosaurs were not large by ancient lizard standards, being under 4 m long. They had porpoise-like heads with a long, toothed snout. Their streamlined shape probably allowed them to swim at about 40 km/h. Although they lived in the oceans, like all lizards they were air breathing and so had to keep coming to the surface. They did not come ashore to lay eggs like many reptiles, but gave birth to live young.

Ichthyosaurs gradually evolved a dorsal fin, even though they were in no way related to fish. It is just one of those things that fast underwater swimming creatures all need to stay upright. The fin contained no bones and so it was a long time before scientists realised that the fin existed.

Ichthyosaurs also had feet (known as paddles) adapted to moving through the water. The paddles were not used to propel the ichthyosaur, however. Instead, it swept its tail from side to side, rather like a shark does.

Ichthyosaurs were hunters, especially of squid-like creatures called belemnites. Early ichthyosaurs could have crushed shells. They also had very large eyes and may have hunted at night.

At the end of the Triassic there was a major change in the world's climate, which killed off many groups of animals. But the ichthyosaurs (like the dinosaurs) survived. After this, with much of the competition extinct, there were lots of opportunities for the ichthyosaurs to evolve to live in all kinds of environments (just as dinosaurs were

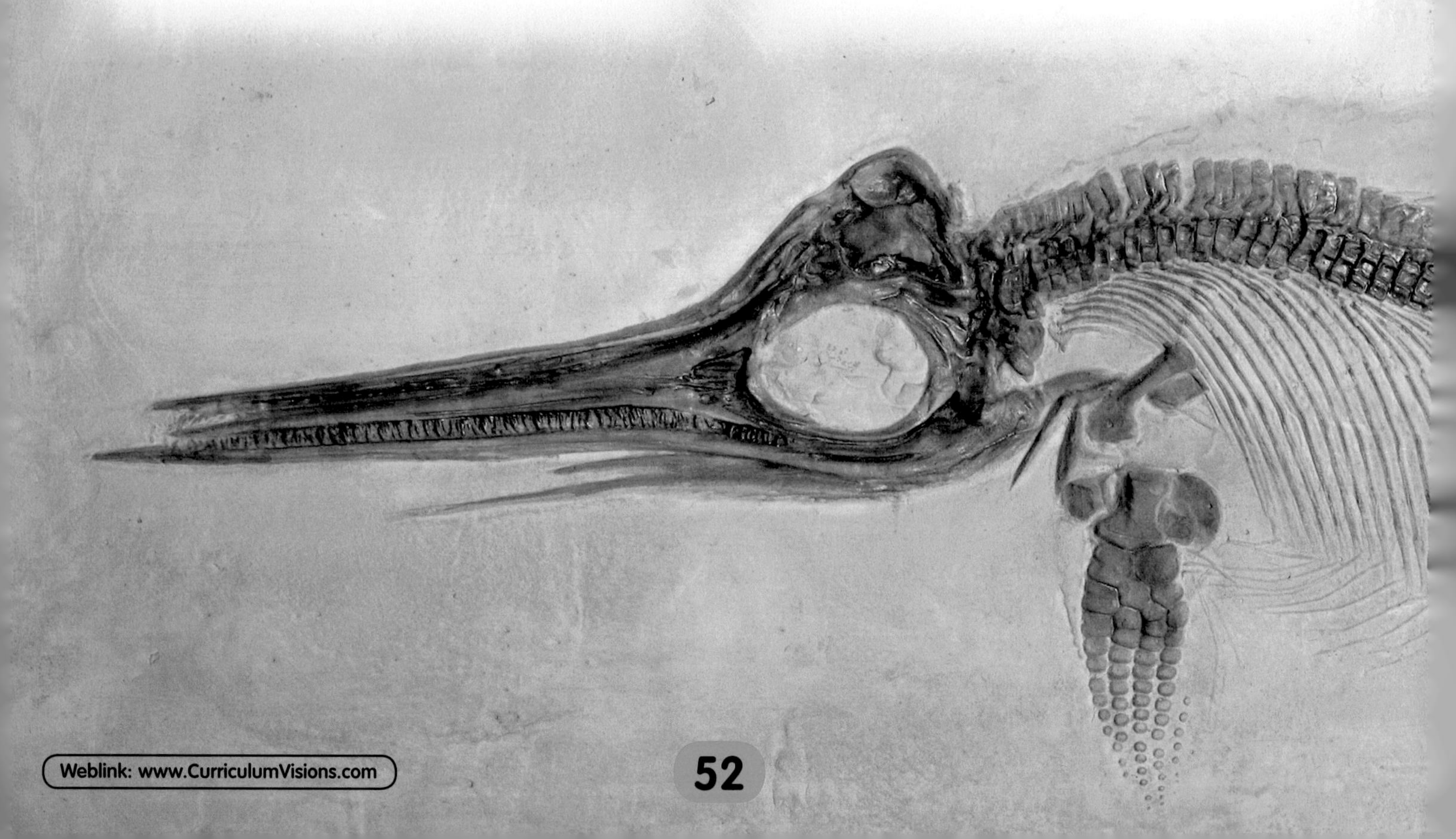

doing on land). This is why they were so varied and abundant in the Jurassic period.

They became less common in the Cretaceous and this may have been because they did not evolve as quickly as their food. By the Cretaceous period, fish, for example, were becoming faster and could more easily outmanoeuvre an ichthyosaur.

Plesiosaurs

Plesiosaurs (meaning 'nearly a lizard') were hunting sea reptiles. True plesiosaurs had long-necks (for example, Elasmosaurus, see pages 50–51) while their relatives, pliosaurs, were short-necked and large-headed. Pliosaurs were much more successful hunters because their shorter necks meant they could move more easily. Pliosaurs grew to 15 m. Plesiosaurs and pliosaurs lived throughout the Jurassic and Cretaceous periods and lived at the same time as dinosaurs.

Elasmosaurus was a plesiosaur with an extremely long neck. It lived in the late Cretaceous period (up to 65 million years ago). It was the longest plesiosaur – about 14 m long – and weighed 2 tonnes. Half of its length was neck – made up of 70 bones – more than any other animal in history. Its limbs had evolved into paddles. It had a small head with many sharp teeth.

Its neck was too weak to allow it to rear up out of the water (as in some popular films) and in fact it probably used the neck as a kind of forward rudder.

It was a slow swimmer which ate fish. The long neck would have allowed Elasmosaurus to have drifted below a school of fish then scooped them up. It swallowed small stones in order to help its digestion.

▼ (2) An ichthyosaur skeleton with shading to show what its shape was like. Note the tail and dorsal fin.

Masters of the skies

Many people know the ancient flying reptiles as 'pterodactyls' but, actually, the name for flying reptiles is pterosaur. Pterodactyl is a group name only for short-tailed pterosaurs which includes Pteranodon, Pterodactylus and Quetzalcoatlus.

Pterodactylus

This is the name of the first pterosaur to be identified as a flying reptile. It was a hunter and probably preyed upon fish and other small animals.

Pterodactylus was a relatively small pterosaur, only 2.5 m across its wings. It had a crest on its skull, long claws, and the back of its neck was covered with hair. It had webbed feet.

Pteranodon

Pteranodon means 'toothless wing'. It lived during the late Cretaceous period in North America. It was one of the largest pterosaurs, growing up to 9 m from wing tip to wing tip. Pteranodon had a crest on its head and a toothless beak, similar to those of modern birds. It would have flown in a soaring manner rather like a modern-day albatross. When on the ground it could have walked on all fours or just on hind legs. It may also have been able to swim.

Pterosaurs, meaning 'winged lizards', lived through the whole Age of the Reptiles. They were some of the first reptiles in the late Triassic, and a few of them were the last of the reptiles to become extinct at the end of the Cretaceous. They were the first animals with backbones to be able to fly. Their wings were made of a membrane of skin stretching from the throat to a hugely lengthened fourth finger.

The first pterosaurs had long tails and long jaws filled with sharp teeth. Later groups had shorter tails, and some were even toothless.

Some pterosaurs were tiny and could have perched on a tree branch, while others (such as Quetzalcoatlus) were enormous.

Dinosaurs and pterosaurs were quite closely related. Pterosaurs were the first animals to have hollow bones (like the bones of modern birds) which helped to reduce their weight and so make it easier for them to fly. They also had a breastbone to which the flight muscles were attached, again like modern birds and some dinosaurs. Many pterosaurs also had webbed feet, which may have allowed them to swim.

Pterosaurs were unique in having hair (rather than feathers). This is very important because it suggests that the pterosaurs were warm-blooded not cold-blooded.

When on the ground, most pterosaurs walked on all fours, but a few species walked upright. Some were probably very ungainly walkers, but others, such as the pteradactyls, seem to have been good at walking and even running.

Pterosaurs may have lived in a variety of environments. Those with small feet most likely needed to walk on firm ground, while those with large feet could have been shallow-water waders.

Pterosaurs protected their eggs from other reptiles by burying them in the ground, much as crocodiles do.

The early pterosaurs were small and lived in trees. They did not survive long into the Cretaceous period and only large pterosaurs survived until the end of the Age of Reptiles.

Quetzalcoatlus

Quetzalcoatlus is named after the Aztec feathered-serpent god Quetzalcoatl. It was a long-necked, toothless pterosaur that lived during the late Cretaceous (84–65 million years ago) in tropical wetland areas of North America. It was one of the largest flying animals of all time with a 10 m wingspan.

Its long neck and toothless jaw may have been suited to scooping up fish, or it may have been a scavenger. Quetzalcoatlus probably walked on all fours, and may even have hunted for food on the ground, using its wings just for soaring from one place to another.

Time line of the dinosaurs

What did the first dinosaurs look like? Where did they come from? Which were common at each stage?

We have all heard of dinosaurs, and we all know they lived a long time ago. But when people talk of dinosaurs they also often use words like Jurassic – for example in the film *Jurassic Park*. So what do words like this mean, and what have they got to do with dinosaurs? To understand this, we have to know something about the history of the Earth.

The Earth is old – very, very old. About 4.6 billion years old to be precise. At first its surface was molten, then covered with volcanoes. There was no oxygen in the air and no oceans at all. But then things began to change. The Earth got cooler and the water, which had come out of volcanoes as gas, began to form droplets of rain that, over hundreds of millions of years, gave us our oceans.

The first living things

These oceans were not such harsh places to live as the air, and their temperatures were much more steady, so this is where the first living things grew (some are still alive today, see background picture). The earliest were very simple – just microscopic simple celled creatures like bacteria and tiny little plants called algae. They began about 3 billion years ago. Over billions more years, these creatures changed and became more complex. We call this natural change **EVOLUTION**.

The first fossils

By about 600 million years ago, evolution had made it possible for living things to develop hard shells (picture ②). These shells did not rot away quickly like fleshy parts of bodies, so there was time for them to be changed into stone – to be made into fossils. That is why we suddenly find fossils at this time.

Making the time line

Evolution produces new and different animals as well as causing some to stop living – to become extinct. That is very different from the way that the Earth's rocks form. They have always formed the same way. So there is not much difference between a sandstone rock that was formed a billion years ago to one formed ten million years ago. This means that if we look for a kind of Earth clock, it's no good looking to the rocks because they don't change. But living things do.

About 200 years ago, people began to realise this and so they started to try to work out the Earth's history and make a time line. They looked hard at the fossils and gradually they found that it was easy to spot some kinds of fossils because they appeared everywhere. They also noticed that each thing lived for a limited range of time. So they started to use fossils to measure time.

Now with fossils used this way, you don't get an actual date, you get a geological 'period'. What you notice through the history of the Earth is that there are long times – periods – when things change gradually, followed by sudden great catastrophes when many creatures are killed off and the land opened up for new ones to take their place, almost like wiping the slate clean. So people studying the rocks – geologists – divided the Earth's history up into periods of calm separated by catastrophes.

Naming the periods

Scientists also found that some places were better for finding fossils than others. So they went to places that were best, and there they started to work. But then they wondered what to call these periods in Earth history that they had found. So they often named the periods after good places for finding the fossils. That is how words like Jurassic came to be. Jurassic is named after the Jura mountains on the border between France and Switzerland where the fossils of that period were first studied.

So now you know how all the funny names came to be. Since then geologists have found ways of knowing how many millions of years the rocks are too, but the period names have stuck.

▼ (2) A trilobite, one of the first living things with a hard shell. This trilobite is 500 million years old.

When the dinosaurs lived

The dinosaurs lived in three of these periods. The oldest period when they lived is called the **TRIASSIC**, the middle one is called the **JURASSIC** and the most recent one is called the **CRETACEOUS** (pronounced kret-ay-shee-us).

Triassic dinosaurs

This period started just after a catastrophe which wiped out two thirds of all living things. But it is an ill wind that blows nobody any good, as they say, and with less competition about, the reptiles evolved quickly into all kinds of shapes and sizes.

Dinosaurs were not the first reptiles to live on Earth. Many species of lizard had already evolved and competed with the first dinosaurs which stopped them from dominating the world.

One of the largest reptile-like creatures still alive was Placerias, a very large plant-eater, up to 4 m long and weighing up to 2 tonnes. It had a beak, rather than a toothed mouth, and short tusks to defend itself. In some ways it was like an armoured hippo and it spent much of its time in the water, in part, perhaps, to keep away from crocodile-like hunters, such as Postosuchus. Postosuchus was the largest hunting dinosaur of the day, being about 6 metres long and 2 metres tall.

But it was not alone. Eoraptor (which means 'dawn plunderer') was also one of the world's earliest dinosaurs. It is possible that the ancestors of all dinosaurs looked like this. This early dinosaur had five fingers on each hand. Three fingers had claws.

Other early hunting dinosaurs included Celophysis and Utahraptor. Meanwhile ichthyosaurs ruled the oceans and the pterosaurs began to fly in the skies.

At this time much of the land was a tropical semi-desert, much like Arizona or Kenya today. It is not an inviting land unless you are adapted to survive in droughts and eat poor, scrubby plants. Like most places with seasonal rain, most animals range around a reliable source of water, such as a waterhole or river bed. During the dry season, venturing to the waterholes and muddy river beds, or trying to eat some of the few remaining plants is much more dangerous. Plant-eaters had to spend all day eating just to stay alive and that means they were easy for the hunters to ambush. Of course, it all depends on size. If you are a plant-eater and you are simply too big to be eaten by a hunter, then you have a great advantage. Thus, natural selection may have favoured the larger, plant-eating dinosaurs.

At the very end of the Triassic period, the single great continent that had existed through early dinosaur times began to split apart (picture ③). It was at this time that many of the competitors of dinosaurs became extinct, leaving the way for dinosaurs to evolve quickly and fill all of the spaces left by their now dead competitors.

◀ ③ During the time of the dinosaurs, the Earth's crust began to split apart, so instead of one giant continent there were many. This was the end of the time of the same species all over the world. From now on species on different continents would evolve separately.

Jurassic dinosaurs

Now there were several smaller continents and they were surrounded with oceans. So it was easier for moisture to reach the land, it rained more and a wider range of plants grew, dominated by dense forests of conifer trees and open plains with fern trees. As there was more food for plant-eating dinosaurs, they increased in number. This, in turn, gave more food for hunting dinosaurs so they increased in number, too.

It was during the Jurassic that some dinosaurs grew into giants. One of the most common was a gentle monster called Diplodocus. It is a member of the sauropods. Other giant sauropods living at the time were Apatosaurus and Brachiosaurus. The main hunters of the age were Allosaurus and Ceratosaurus.

The Jurassic truly was the age of the dinosaurs. Of course, individual species did not survive the whole of the time, and some became extinct, while new species evolved. For example, Stegosaurus became extinct at the end of the Jurassic (picture ④).

At the same time, the reptiles in the oceans became ever more common. They included ichthyosaurs, plesiosaurs and crocodiles.

Cretaceous dinosaurs

The Cretaceous was also a time of change, and many new dinosaurs evolved (picture ⑤).

Because contents had split apart, animals evolved differently on the separate continents. So species found on one continent are not found on another. For this reason, the Cretaceous saw more variety in dinosaurs than ever before. This is why the kinds of Tyrannosaurus found in North America are different from the Tyrannosaurus species in Asia (called Tarbosaurus), for example. Other famous dinosaurs were plant-eaters such as Triceratops and Zuniceratops.

But competition was setting in as birds evolved from dinosaur ancestors and competed against the pterosaurs, which gradually became extinct.

This change was not all good for dinosaurs. New kinds of plants – flowering plants, including broad-leaved trees – were evolving and dinosaurs were not evolving fast enough to eat this new food. Many dinosaurs faded away during the Cretaceous.

But then, as in so many times in the past, and presumably as will happen in the future, there was a catastrophe that changed the world. About 65 million years ago a comet crashed into the Earth somewhere around what is now the Gulf of Mexico in America. Huge clouds of dust were thrown up and the climate cooled. Many plants died, so there was less food for the plant-eating dinosaurs. That in turn meant there was less meat for the hunting dinosaurs and so they died out too. The time was over for the dinosaurs.

They may well have perished especially because they were so big and needed so much food. But, whatever the cause, without the dinosaurs in the early years of the Tertiary period that followed the Cretaceous, a small number of mammals were able to find enough food and thrive, evolving to take over the land once ruled by dinosaurs. And those mammals eventually evolved – into, amongst others, you and me.

◀ ④ Stegosaurus, a plant-eating dinosaur of the Jurassic.

▶ ⑤ Spinosaurus was a Cretaceous hunter.

The missing link?

Dinosaurs are present today in the form of animals like crocodiles and birds. We are not their direct descendants. But, curiously enough, some of our possible descendants were around probably in the age of dinosaurs and may well have seen T. rex stomping over the plains.

Quite recently, one of these mammals – the missing link, as it has been called – has been found as a complete skeleton. It has been dated to 47 million years ago. That is about 20 million years after the dinosaurs became extinct, but nothing much in evolutionary terms. This one was possibly like a modern lemur and lived in trees, using its long tail for balancing as it did a tight-rope act along the branches.

The animal is a missing link insofar as it is the oldest specimen that can be called a primate (like us) that has yet been found. It is called Darwinius masillae (after Charles Darwin and the place in Germany, called Messel, where the specimen was found). However, it is popularly known as Ida. It is about 60 cm long, or roughly the size of a small, long-tailed cat. It has grasping hands with opposable thumbs, and nails instead of claws.

◀▶ Compare the skeleton of Ida with the dinosaur skeletons on earlier pages to see the differences. In particular, look at the hands.

Glossary

CERATOPSIA Horn-faced plant-eating dinosaurs.

CONTINENTAL DRIFT The gradual movement of the continents over geological time. It usually refers to a time starting in the Jurassic.

CRETACEOUS The fourth period of the Mesozoic Era, after the Jurassic. When the continents began to split up and dinosaurs evolved separately on each continent.

EVOLUTION The way living things change over time.

EXTINCT/EXTINCTION When all the living members of a species die out.

FOSSIL The remains of a long-dead living thing. Fossils can be in the form of mineralised bones and tissues, carbon deposits or even impressions.

GEOLOGICAL AGE A time of the Earth's past. The most commonly used words are era and period. An era is a very long time: all of the time of the dinosaurs fit inside the Mesozoic Era. A geological period is shorter – a time between major Earth changes. The Triassic, Jurassic and Cretaceous periods make up most of the Mesozoic Era.

HADROSAUR Bird-like dinosaurs.

JURASSIC The third period of the Mesozoic Era, after the Triassic when the continents began to split up and dinosaurs evolved separately on each continent.

PANGEA The name give to an ancient continent that existed at the start of the time of the dinosaurs. At this time there was only a single, gigantic continent – Pangea – on Earth. Then, in the Jurassic, it began to split up to give the continents we know today.

REPTILE Cold-blooded animal with scales and which lays eggs. Many people believe dinosaurs were not true reptiles and that many were warm-blooded. Nevertheless, the popular term for 'The Age of Dinosaurs' is often 'The Age of Reptiles'.

SAUROPOD Large plant-eating dinosaurs.

THEROPOD Large hunting, meat-eating dinosaurs.

TITANOSAUR The last great group of gigantic sauropods that replaced Jurassic sauropods like Diplodocus during Cretaceous times. Strangly, few remains of them have been found.

TRIASSIC The second period of the Mesozoic Era (after the Permian in which there were no dinosaurs).

Index